A Gaia **Busy Person's** Guide

Tai Chi

A Gaia **Busy Person's** Guide

Tai Chi

Simple routines for home, work, & travel

Tin-Yu LAM

Gaia Books

A Gaia Original

Books from Gaia celebrate the vision of Gaia, the self-sustaining living Earth, and seek to help its readers live in greater personal and planetary harmony.

Editorial Cathy Meeus, Jo Godfrey Wood
Designer Bridget Morley
Photography Paul Forrester
Production Aileen O'Reilly
Direction Jo Godfrey Wood, Patrick Nugent

® This is a Registered Trade Mark of Gaia Books

First published in the United Kingdom in 2005 by
Gaia Books, 2–4 Heron Quays, London E14 4JP

ISBN 1 85675 207 0
EAN 9 781856 752077

A catalogue record of this book is available from the British Library

Printed and bound in China

10 9 8 7 6 5 4 3 2 1

CAUTION
The techniques, ideas and suggestions in this book are to be used at the reader's sole discretion and risk. Always follow the instructions carefully, observe the cautions and consult a doctor if in doubt about a medical condition.

Contents

About the author

Tin-Yu Lam was born in England in 1978. He is the second son of Master Lam Kam-Chuen, who is a respected international authority on a wide range of Chinese arts.

The traditional Chinese way is for the sons to inherit the knowledge and expertise of their fathers. Tin-Yu Lam and his brothers studied under Master Lam from a very early age, as a member of a highly traditional and very cultured family environment. Tin-Yu studied Tai Chi Chuan, Chi Kung and a number of other Chinese arts. His style of Tai Chi Chuan is based upon his father's lifelong understanding and refinement of the art, popularly known as Lam-style Tai Chi Chuan.

From a young age Tin-Yu developed a genuine interest in all things ancient. In his pursuit, he studied world mythology and ancient philosophy, mainly the Eastern philosophies; in particular Buddhism, Taoism and the I Ching.

Tin-Yu Lam graduated from Imperial College with a BSc in Mathematics and Management and a Masters Degree in Finance. He is currently a futures trader in Canary Wharf, London. His first book, *The Way of Tea*, was a joint production with his parents and has been distributed internationally in several languages.

Using this book

The traditional way to study Tai Chi Chuan (the formal name for Tai Chi) was to practise under the guidance of a master for several hours each day. This old ideal of rising with the sun and then training with the crowing of the rooster, however, is a rare occurrence today. The purpose of this book is to accommodate the study and practice of the art of Tai Chi within the time-poor lifestyle of many of us in today's industrialised world, without losing the colour and the content of the art.

This book is suitable for both beginners and those who are already acquainted with Tai Chi. I have carefully selected a range of Tai Chi exercises and techniques that you can incorporate into your busy lifestyle, with minimum disruption. It is designed to be a daily programme of exercise.

Chinese culture has very firm views on practice, meditation, training and education. They are all regarded as a form of 'cultivation'. Studying is considered to be a cultivation of the mind, as physical training is a cultivation of the body. To maintain the fruits of cultivation, the Chinese say: 'Learning is sailing against the current. If [you are] not progressing, [you] must therefore be regressing.'

What this really means is that if you learn Tai Chi Chuan but do not practise, all that you have is a pale and incomplete reflection of this art form. So, remember – learn and practise as much as you can.

Introduction

Knowledge of Tai Chi Chuan (referred to from now on as Tai Chi) has spread widely in recent decades, yet there are many popular misconceptions about its exact nature. Sometimes termed a 'soft' martial art, it is one of the few great physical art forms that have been passed down from ancient civilisations to today, from generation to generation, as a continuous, unbroken thread, unaffected by time. By studying Tai Chi under the trained eyes of a master, you maintain its unbroken lineage.

The name Tai Chi (meaning 'the supreme ultimate') is borrowed from one of the three major philosophies in China – Taoism. As well as having the practical applications of any martial art, Tai Chi is said to promote longevity, refine the mind and help balance.

TAI CHI'S EVER-EVOLVING NATURE

Because of the nature of Chinese teaching systems – from father to son and master to student – Tai Chi is a truly organic art form. From its earliest days, exceptional masters have contributed their wisdom and insights. And with their modifications, Tai Chi has evolved into the many different schools and forms of today. Although no two masters teach the system in exactly the same way, the basic principles of Tai Chi remain constant.

Tai Chi is suitable for all ages, young and old, but it has become especially popular among older people. Today in China (and in Chinese communities around the world) it is quite usual to see groups of senior citizens gathered together in the public parks and open spaces of large cities in the early morning to practise Tai Chi.

MYSTERIOUS ORIGINS

The exact origins of Tai Chi is a mystery and will probably remain so. Some evidence suggests that an early form of Tai Chi was taught and practised as early as the third century BCE. Many scholars have researched the subject but have been unable to find any conclusive evidence of its origins, nor have they been able to agree with one another. The relative obscurity of Tai Chi's origins lies mainly with the system of education in ancient China.

Knowledge has always been considered sacred in the East and was, therefore, treated with much reverence. Open knowledge was a rarity. People learned their trades or crafts under some form of apprenticeship system. Education was a closed, intimate and sometimes secretive process. The teacher–student relationship was considered of equal importance, and sometimes superior even to that between a father and a son.

The teaching and practice of the martial arts also fell under this closed education system. Those who were expert in the art of Tai Chi treated it with great reverence and recognised its marvels, guarding its secrets closely. Fathers taught their sons in secret and very little was put into writing. It is the continuous practice of oral instruction that brings Tai Chi to the world today.

THE STORY OF CHANG SAN-FENG

Many theories have been proposed about the origin of Tai Chi, but by far the most popular, and most loved, is the tale of Chang San-Feng.

Chang San-Feng is said to have lived in the 14th century, some time between the end of the Yuan and the beginning of the Ming dynasties. He was a Buddhist monk living and studying in the renowned Shaolin Temple. For various reasons and after some adventures, Chang San-Feng came to find Buddhism unsatisfactory and began to search for another religious framework. He became involved in the practice of Shaolin Kung Fu – a hard and rigid discipline. Strength, force and power were the qualities emphasised by the martial arts of his time.

Chang San-Feng's search for another philosophy led him to Taoism, the native religion of China, with its concepts of Yin and Yang and the Five Elements (earth, air, fire, water and metal). He decided to utilise the yin–yang philosophy and apply it to the martial arts. He became a Taoist priest and retreated to Wu-Tang Mountain, where he created a school for teaching his new system of martial arts.

Chang San-Feng introduced the revolutionary element of 'softness' to the discipline – a dramatic and significant change of view in the martial arts world of the time. Tai Chi soon became famous for this softness and the Chinese martial arts tradition of Kung Fu was never the same again.

Though this legend may lack historical authenticity and the actual existence of Chang San-Feng is questionable, it is the best-loved Tai Chi myth. It is coloured with the romance and historical significance of Wu-Tang and Shaolin, the two great martial arts establishments of ancient China with their two different philosophies – Taoism and Buddhism, the two rival yet complementary religions of China.

In the more fanciful legends, Chang San-Feng was said to have lived an extraordinarily long life. The link between longevity and Tai Chi was therefore established. Whether or not Chang San-Feng really existed, he has remained a much-respected figure in Chinese history. The authorship of the ancient manuscript *Tai Chi Chuan Classics* has been attributed to him. Upon this manuscript was a note stating:

> *This classic was left by the patriarch*
> *Chang San-Feng of Wu-Tang Mountain.*
> *He desired the whole world to attain longevity,*
> *and not only martial techniques.*

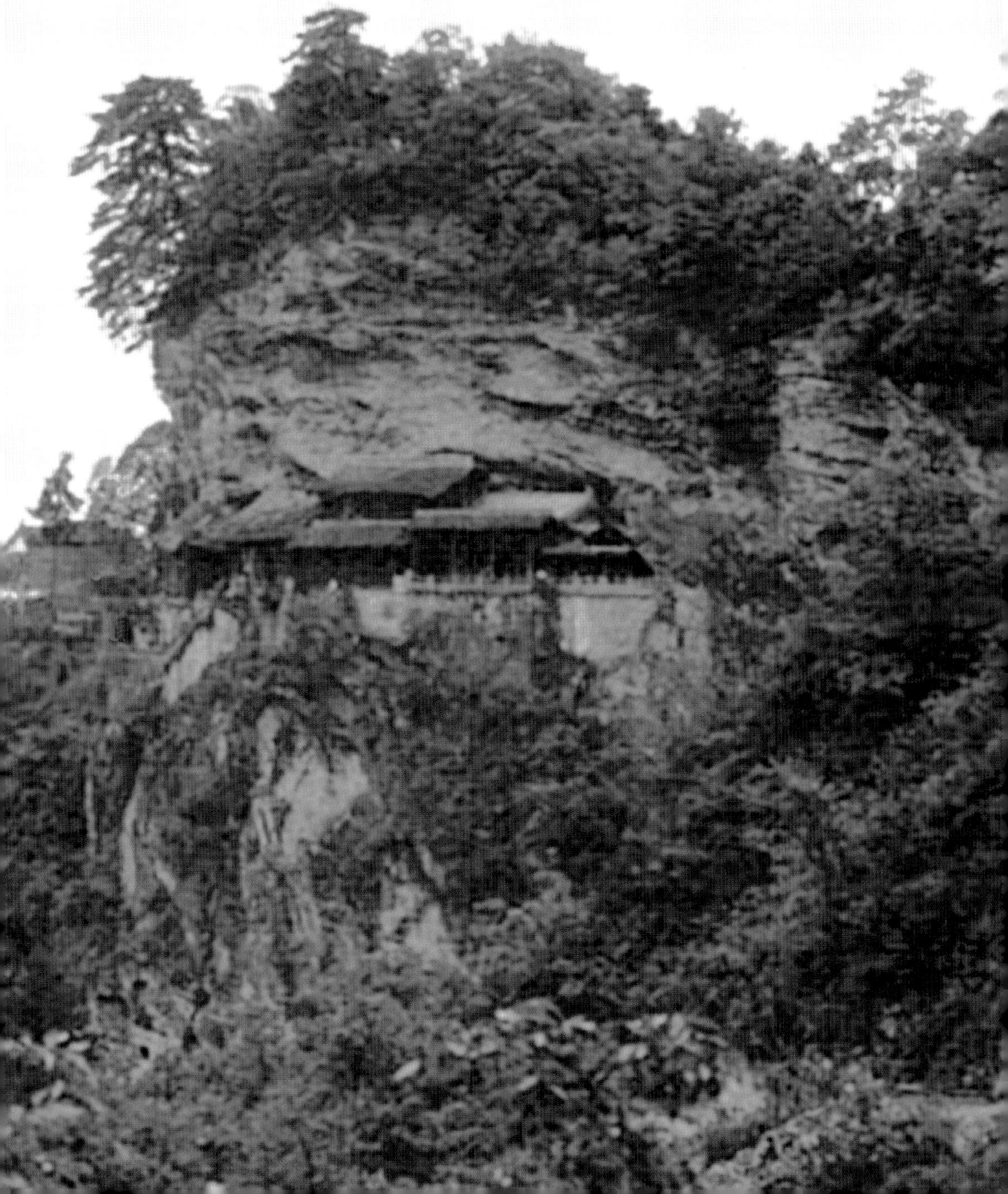

CHAPTER ONE

What is Tai Chi?

Tai Chi, meaning literally 'the supreme
ultimate', is a term borrowed from Taoism,
the principal philosophy and religion of China.
Tai Chi is, in essence, an application of the
Taoist principles to martial arts.

In its most basic application Tai Chi is one of the most effective all-round physical exercise systems. With its carefully balanced postures and its emphasis on slow, flowing movements, it encourages physical fitness, coordination and suppleness without the risk of strain or injury. It is a form of exercise that can be practised by people of all ages, whatever their fitness level. Its stimulating effects on the circulation and gentle toning of the muscles helps to improve energy levels and stamina. Its meditative qualities also make it a perfect antidote to the psychological stresses of modern living, helping to induce relaxation, which in turn improves the functioning of all the body's systems as well as boosting mental acuity and powers of concentration.

While its origins are mysterious and ancient, Tai Chi is ideally suited to a busy modern lifestyle. It does not require a rigid training programme and elements of it can be practised virtually anywhere and at any time, without the need for equipment or special clothing.

Tai Chi can be undertaken on a basic level and provides many benefits without the need for any engagement in its philosophical origins. Most practitioners of this art, however, find that their practice is enhanced by a basic understanding of the Taoist concepts on which it was founded. An appreciation of these ideas, outlined on the following pages, helps to explain the principles behind and the aims of the Tai Chi exercises that you will learn.

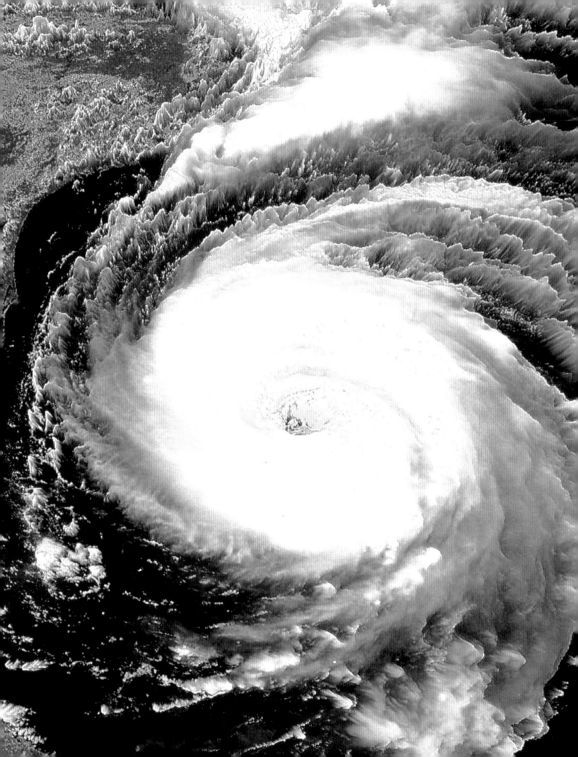

Yin and Yang

To understand Tai Chi, it is helpful to begin with the twin principles of Tao – Yin and Yang. The complete mastery and understanding of Yin and Yang is said to be the domain of gods and demi-gods, but it is also the lifelong study of many priests, scholars and holy men. Below is a brief description of the complex concepts of Yin and Yang and their inter-relationships.

Yin and Yang are the two harmonious yet conflicting forces or principles that dictate all aspects of life. As they are meant to encompass the breadth of all things in existence, the twin principles of Yin and Yang can be seen expressed in innumerable forms.

In their most basic form Yin and Yang refer to darkness and light, respectively. The archetypal image of Yang is the sun – literally, the Grand Yang in Chinese; whereas the moon – the Grand Yin – is the archetypal image of Yin.

The Yin principle encompasses the qualities of dark, earth, water and the feminine, while Yang has the qualities of light, heaven, fire and the masculine. Their expressions, or manifestations, are wide-ranging and colourful. For example, if Yin is manifest as a tiger, then Yang is a dragon. In terms of numbers, Yin represents even numbers while Yang the odd numbers. Whatever the manifestation, Yin and Yang are always the opposite of each other, existing only with the presence of their counterparts.

GRAPHIC REPRESENTATIONS

The pictorial symbol for Yang is a simple horizontal line; for Yin, the horizontal line is broken into two segments. These are the standardised symbols for the two primal forces as given in I Ching, the *Book of Change*. You may also come across other, more ancient, representations, with Yang represented as a horizontal line and Yin ranging from a broken line to a reversed 'V'. There is no equivalent representation of these fundamental ideas in Western language or any Western philosophy.

Yang

Yin

The Chinese written characters of Yin and Yang are complex; each expressing some of the qualities of the other principle. Both characters depict sunlight shining on two sides of a hill – one side is bathed in light, while the other is cloaked in darkness. The Yin character depicts people under a roof and a cloud, representing obscurity and shadow, whereas the Yang character includes a representation of moving energy and a sun above the horizon, indicating brightness.

YIN–YANG AND TAI CHI

In a martial arts context the principles of Yin and Yang can represent soft and hard, slow and fast, offensive and defensive, invading and yielding, yourself and the opponent and much more. The balanced and comprehensive application of the Yin and Yang principles is the very essence of Tai Chi.

The calligraphy on the scroll on the facing page represents Yin (top) and Yang (below).

Existence and non-existence

According to Taoist thinking, at its most basic level, the source of existence is 'non-existence'. This absence of existence is also sometimes called 'void' or 'nothingness'. It is not simply a physical vacuum as in terms of an absence of material and physical particles, but it is a philosophical nothingness, referring to the absolute absence of anything, whether physical, spiritual, imaginary or conceptual. This foremost and most fundamental principle to the order of things is termed Wu Chi, and it is graphically depicted as an empty circle – a shape implying an unchanging continuity, which is hollow inside.

The next principle to the order of all things is existence – also known as You Chi. According to this concept all things are fundamentally identical. The 'myriad things' in the universe are simply existence (this is similar to the Western concept of unity). The pictorial representation of You Chi is an empty circle with a dot at its centre.

After this comes the system of Yin and Yang. These two primal forces are together portrayed as a circle, half filled in black and half in white. These orders of principles can be expressed numerically, as in Tao Te Ching:

'Tao bore One.
One bore Two.
Two bore Three.
Three bore Myriad Things.'

THE TWO EXTREMES

Each level of these principles is important when you are studying Taoism. In this context, Yin and Yang are termed Liang Chi, meaning the two extremes. They are called extremes because they express concepts that have no ending or finality but are simply two opposite directions of ideas.

A simple analogy would be left and right. Left and right are two mutually dependent, but opposite, concepts. Turning left, there is always more room for one to turn left again. The goal of left exists in one sense, yet is unreachable. The same is true for right.

The entire system of Yin and Yang and their various inter-relations are collectively and singularly called Tai Chi, the Grand Extreme or Supreme Ultimate.

Chi

This term is heard frequently in the context of Chinese culture and philosophy. This *chi* (unrelated to the one in the name Tai Chi) is sometimes spelled 'qi' and may be translated as 'breath', 'energy' or 'aura'.

THE NATURE OF *CHI*

The concept of *chi* is used in a whole range of subjects, from medicine to cookery. The idea of *chi* is one of the backbones of Chinese culture and thinking. It is the underlying and fundamental 'substance' that everything contains and is composed of. It is the fundamental and vital force of all things – inanimate or living. *Chi* exists everywhere and in everything. It is shapeless and formless, moving like fluid or gas – sometimes growing, sometimes subsiding.

Another way of approaching the concept of *chi* is through the idea of existence. All things – material and immaterial – come under the heading of 'existence'. For example, while a wave has no distinct physical properties, being simply the result of the action of winds and tides on water, its existence is unquestionable. *Chi* can be thought of in the same way, but it carries a much wider application.

In Taoism the properties of all things, the change of properties of things and the

The top character represents Tai and the lower one Chi.

interactions between things are all explained in terms of the changes and movements in the state of *chi*. *Chi* is everywhere and exists within everything, from the material and physical to immaterial concepts such as fortune and fame.

CHI AND TAI CHI

In Tai Chi, *chi* refers to the invisible medium of strength, energy and power that exists within everyone. The acupuncture point called Tan Tien, which is located approximately 5 cm (2 in) below the navel, is the core of the human *chi* system.

When practising Tai Chi, it is important to stimulate your *chi* while you are carrying out the exercises; you should feel it consciously and intuitively. This contrasts with the normally dormant state of *chi* during everyday activities. After the *chi* has been stimulated, your aim is to guide it down the body into your Tan Tien. This conscious manipulation of *chi* is one of the many goals in the effective practice of Tai Chi.

There are many ways you can manipulate *chi* and being thoroughly aware of your *chi* throughout the movements and stillness of Tai Chi is something to aspire to. But, it's vital that you do not deviate from the fundamental point of exciting and concentrating the *chi* at the Tan Tien – it is important to bear this in mind when you are trying out the exercises.

Shen

If you look up *shen* in a Chinese–English dictionary, you will probably find that it means 'god' or 'divine', but this definition does not apply here. *Shen* is not a philosophical concept like *chi* or Yin–Yang but is a literal term. The term *shen* used in martial arts refers to something of the spirit and the mind and there is no exact translation in English. *Shen* is the invisible force that governs the state of the human mind. Below are some common allusions to *shen* in Chinese thought.

* When you feel refreshed, the *shen* is refined.
* When you are concentrating, the refined *shen* is gathered to the centre.
* When you are depressed, your *shen* and *chi* are absent.
* If you become irrational, your *shen* and spirit are overturned.

THE EXPRESSION OF *SHEN*

From these examples, you can see that the *shen* is neither mind nor spirit – it is simply an intuitive expression of your state of mind and can be described as the 'substance' of the mind. It is the medium in which the state of one's spirit resides and the medium that generates the expression on one's face.

The calligraphy for Shen.

SHEN
A person practising Tai Chi seems to display an inner radiance, a readiness to act, a preparedness and a certain quality of majesty, which is known as shen.

Therefore, when an observer looks at the *shen* of another person, he or she looks at the expressions reflected in the face – especially the eyes – and the mood that is shown there. However, the expressions themselves are not important; they are secondary to the primary source of these physiological effects.

SHEN IN TAI CHI

When you are practising Tai Chi, a good description of the state of your mind is that it should be 'vivid'. This vividness is not the same as the bubbling liveliness of a child when she sees a new toy. It is more like that air of might and majesty that we can see in great leaders. The *shen* should radiate an air of erupting inaction, rather like a drawn bow or the calm before the storm. You can see it more plainly in the animal kingdom during fighting or hunting.

Tai Chi, however, aims for a more refined state of *shen* than the raw and primitive equivalent exhibited by beasts and birds in the natural world. The *shen* should also be focused and collected, relaxed yet excited. These qualities may seem contradictory if you are new to the art of Tai Chi, but it is this balance between opposing forces that is at its very essence.

'*I*'

The simplest translation of *i* (pronounced 'ee') is 'the will'. This concept entails a combination of your will and your thoughts, with the emphasis upon the will. Its importance in the practice of Tai Chi is that the true essence of this art lies within you and is not based on your external appearance. Your external qualities are secondary and are the direct results of the inner effects of your Tai Chi practice.

THOUGHTS SURPASS VISION

In China, there is an ancient proverb that says that having many legs is not necessarily better than having no legs at all; that the formlessness of clouds and wind is faster than the fleet of feet; that the power of sight surpasses the swiftness of wind; and that thoughts surpass vision.

Given the swiftness of thoughts, it is easy to understand why it is said that the involvement of the will – *i* – comes into play before the physical movements and sequences of Tai Chi. The *i* comes before the *chi*, which in turns comes before the actions of the body: *i* moves first and the body moves last. If it does not, then the practice is without purpose – it is nothing but shallow, meaningless body movements and shapes, and this is not Tai Chi.

Think of a train. The *i* is the engine at the front, which provides the moving force for the rest of the train. The body, and its actions, is the last carriage and its role is simply to follow.

The calligraphy for 'I'.

Sum

The calligraphy for Sum.

Sum can be directly translated as 'the heart'. But, there is a cultural difference surrounding the idea of the word 'heart' between the East and the West. In the West, the heart is regarded as the source of human emotions, especially in relation to romantic love. It is seen as the origin and dwelling place of human love and hatred. In the East, it refers to the mind or the soul. Therefore, the Western phrase 'body and mind' or 'body and soul' is more accurately translated as 'body and heart' in the East. So, when you refer to the mind in Tai Chi, you should visualise it in the heart rather than the head.

CLARITY OF HEART

When you are practising Tai Chi your mind needs to stay calm. But this is a very different kind of calmness than that which is generally understood in the West; it is much more than just an absence of tension. The Chinese terminology reflects this significant difference. The word for calm in Chinese is *ching* meaning 'clarity' and 'purity' and the literal Chinese phrase is 'clarity of heart'. It not only refers to mental and emotional stability, as suggested in its Western equivalent, but also describes a state of being. A popular Chinese metaphor for this has always been the transparency and purity of clean water: even if you shake it up violently, it remains entirely and constantly clear.

The Tai Chi lifestyle

Tai Chi is the application of the philosophy of Taoism in martial arts. However, the opposite is equally true. To many scholars and priests, the purpose of the practice of Tai Chi is to gain further insights into the workings of existence and the philosophy of Tao. With the right amount of attention and dedication, Tai Chi is as much a spiritual and mental medium as it is a martial art. This philosophy may well be beyond your aims of what you hope to gain when reading and using this book, but it can help your practice within your busy schedule to bear in mind that you can think of all aspects of daily life as a form of Tai Chi.

A MIDDLE WAY

For most of us the main objective is to find a balanced and constructive middle way rather than an extreme. This is very closely associated with the Buddhist idea of 'moderation in all things'. You should not have too much or too little. Standing in the middle and taking advantages of both sides is, in Tai Chi terms, the correct and moderate way to behave.

This is how Tai Chi was incorporated into the lives of scholars and priests of ancient China. In terms of eating and diet, you should try not to favour a particular food or taste. In terms of opinions, you should be open to understanding both sides of an argument or discussion. Your leisure and work should be balanced and, in general, nothing should be either excessive or lacking. Balance and moderation in all things is Tai Chi's way to a healthy and good lifestyle.

If you do not have a balanced and harmonious lifestyle, no end of practising Tai Chi will offer you great things. Any benefits you gain from your Tai Chi practice will be diminished and, at worst, negated by an unhealthy lifestyle. This comes as no great surprise since your Tai Chi practice takes up only a small part of your life, while your lifestyle dictates and dominates you all day, every day.

CHAPTER TWO

At the start of the day

It is amazing what a few minutes of Tai Chi each morning can do for your body and mind. Make it part of your daily morning routine – like taking a shower and brushing your teeth.

In the modern world, our daily schedules often deviate from the natural human cycle of getting up and going to bed with the sun. What was once the norm in a simpler age has become all too rare in our typical lifestyles today.

The morning is a vital, if not the most important, time of day in human activities. Most of us appreciate in our daily lives that our mood and physical condition in the morning has repercussions on our state of mind and performance for the rest of the day. This insight, of course, did not escape the sharp eyes and ears of our forefathers and the wisdom has been passed down through the generations. Many major human activities, ranging from education timetables to military decisions, have been based upon this perception.

The morning is the ideal time for the practice of Tai Chi. In China, and in Chinese communities worldwide, the parks are filled with young and old performing Tai Chi movements before the start of the working day. The exercises provide a healthy and energising boost that can make your day's activities more effective. If you are one of the many people who find waking up difficult, surfacing and then drifting back to sleep again despite the fact that the day awaits, a morning routine of breathing exercises and simple movements can help to prepare you for the day ahead. These exercises are not strenuous and some you can even do while you are still in bed.

In bed

You have probably experienced those mornings when the little voice in your head urges you to get up, but your body refuses to listen. If you are a victim of these morning ordeals, the breathing exercises on the facing page and the leg circling exercise on the next may help you make a more energetic start to the day.

First, lie perfectly still on your back. Do not let your body twist to the left or the right. Position your pillow so that it's not too high or too low and position your head, neck and body in alignment in a natural, comfortable position. Don't try to hold your legs together, just let them fall apart naturally.

Do the breathing exercise for several minutes as soon as you wake up, without leaving the cosiness of your bed. Remain perfectly still, but comfortably so. If you experience stiffness in any part of your body, ease it away and release it gently. If you enjoy a certain sleepy idleness in the morning you probably won't find relaxing a problem. Once you have settled yourself into this position, close your eyes and begin the breathing exercise, but try not to fall back to sleep.

You will soon discover that if you have strong legs, you will feel stronger all over. A regular wake-up call for your legs first thing in the morning will help you start the day feeling empowered and ready for the activities ahead. Regular practice of the gentle exercise described on pages 34–35 will also gradually strengthen your legs. Your legs have been 'asleep' for the entire night, so this exercise acts as a gentle wake-up call for them before they start their work for the day – bearing your weight and moving you about.

BREATHING EXERCISE

TIPS
• Each breath should be prolonged and even. Inhale slowly and continuously, taking a series of small units of breath, so that each individual breath lasts as long as possible.

• Breathe in deeply and fully, and exhale at the same slow, soft and even rate. Rest your hands on your belly and feel them rising and falling to the rhythm of your breaths.

• The key words in this practice are:
  • Soft
  • Even
  • Small
  • Slow
  • Deep
  • Gentle
  • Continuous
  • Long

(01) Lie quite still on your back, your elbows resting on the bed and your hands placed lightly at hip level on either side of your Tan Tien (see p.21).

(02) Breathe in. Do not expand your chest. Instead, let your breath sink towards your Tan Tien. Your hands should feel your belly rising with the intake of breath.

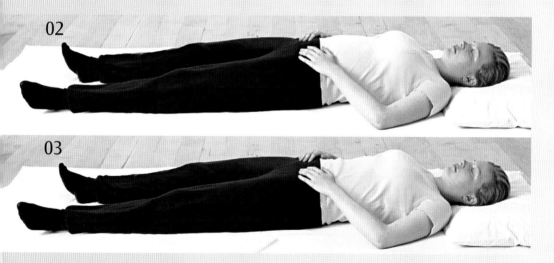

(03) As you breathe out, feel your hands sinking. Continue breathing in this way for several minutes.

LEG EXERCISE

(01) Fold back the bedclothes before you start. Lie on your back and rest your hands lightly on either side of your Tan Tien. Your elbows should rest on the bed on either side of your body.

(02) Raise your right leg by bending your knee towards your upper body. Do not bend the knee so much that it creates tension in your lower body. Allow your upper body, right thigh and lower leg to create a natural step shape and flex the foot. Don't let your leg lean left or right.

01

(03) Now imagine that your right foot is holding an invisible pen between your first and second toes. Rotate your foot clockwise 15–20 times, as if you were drawing circles in the air. Lower your leg to the bed and relax. When you have completed the exercise with your right leg, repeat it with your left leg, but this time circle in an anti-clockwise direction.

TIP
• While circling your foot, move only the lower part of your leg, but allow your thigh to oscillate to the left and right slightly.

02

03

Sitting by the bed

Immediately after you get out of bed, before leaving its side, there are several things you can do to prepare for your day. Either sit on the side of your bed or move to a comfortable bedroom chair. First, try this invigorating facial massage to wake you up properly. Start by rubbing your hands together, as shown right – this produces physical warming and stimulates the flow of *chi*, which boosts the effectiveness of the massage. If your hands cool down during the routine, simply rub them together again for a little longer and then continue from wherever you left off.

WARMING YOUR HANDS

Before you start any massage, warm your hands by rubbing them together firmly but gently. Hold them against each other so that fingers as well as palms make contact. After a short time, hands and fingers should have warmed up completely.

01

FACE MASSAGE

This simple facial massage helps to awaken the mind and keep it alert for the rest of the day. When performed daily, this routine can do wonders for your effectiveness at work.

(01) As soon as your hands are warm, rest the palms on your face and rub gently but firmly 10–15 times in an up-and-down motion.

02

(02) Now change to a circling action, moving your left hand in an anti-clockwise direction and your right hand clockwise. Massage in large circles, taking in your forehead, the sides of your face and your chin. Repeat 10–15 times. Finally, let your hands rest over your face and let your eyes and cheeks absorb their warmth for a few seconds.

KNEE MASSAGE

Begin by warming your hands (see p.36) and place them on your knees. Massage the entire knee area, not just the kneecaps, by circling your left hand in an anti-clockwise direction and your right hand in a clockwise direction. Do this 10–15 times. If your hands cool down partway through, then pause to rub them and restart.

NECK MASSAGE

(01–03) Now it's time to massage the back of your neck. Rub both hands together firmly but gently. Place them on the back of your neck, with fingertips touching. Imagine your hands are like a towel that you use to rub your neck from side to side, covering the back and sides of your neck. Do this 10–15 times.

01

02

03

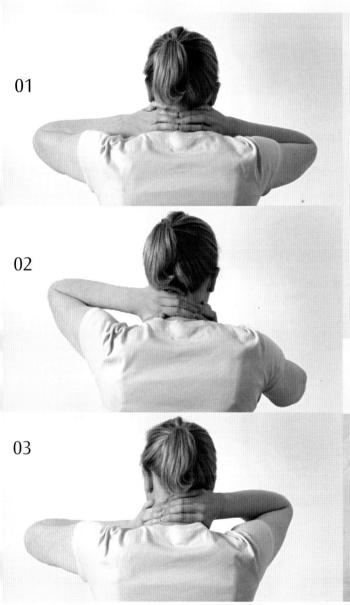

LEG EXERCISE

While you're still sitting by the bed, try this leg exercise. Begin by sitting up straight, with both hands resting on your thighs. With your right foot, draw a large circle on the floor, moving your foot slowly and smoothly in a clockwise direction. Do this 15 times. Don't lift your foot from the floor. Repeat with the left foot, but this time drawing a circle in an anticlockwise direction.

Standing

By now you should feel ready to stand up and try some more vigorous movements. The exercises on the following pages are designed to move your *chi* from deep within your body out to your extremities, preparing your whole body for the activities ahead.

01

(01) *Stand up, remaining relaxed and comfortable, with your legs hip-width apart and your hands resting loosely by your sides. Your knees are slightly bent.*

CROSS HANDS

This exercise helps to mobilise your upper body.

(02) Draw your hands slowly together and cross them in front of your face. Both palms should be facing towards you, with your right hand closest to your face.

(03) Swing your hands in two large arcs down towards your thighs, palms facing down, stopping when they are about hip level.

(04) Then, reverse the movement, swinging your hands back to the cross-hands position. Repeat the whole movement 15–20 times.

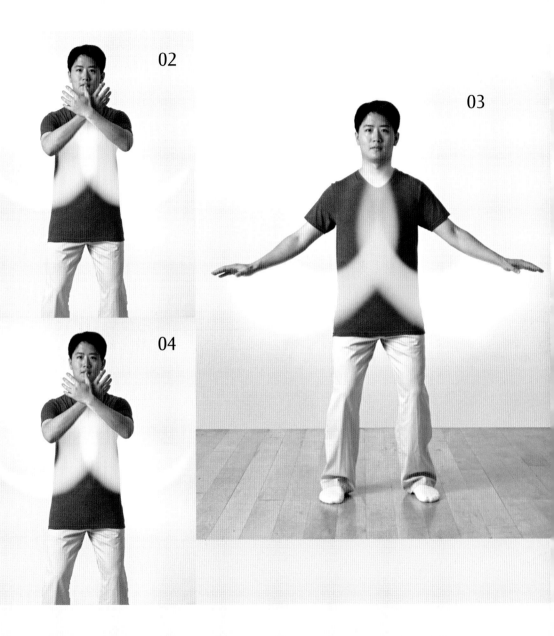

ARM SIDE-SWINGING

Although this is not a traditional Tai Chi gesture, this exercise is very useful for loosening your arms and shoulders and for promoting general coordination – a vital requirement for practising good Tai Chi.

02

01

(01) Start by standing with your body straight and your knees slightly bent. Rest your arms loosely by your sides, palms inwards.

(02) Raise both arms up to your right, until your right arm is fully extended to the side and your left hand is level with your right shoulder. Do not let your left elbow drop. The fingers of both hands should remain straight, but not tense. Both palms should face downwards.

(03) Swing both arms horizontally to the left until they reach a position that mirrors the previous posture. Don't use so much force that your left arm is thrown too far back. Keep the palms down throughout.

(04) Next, swing your arms back to your right and continue to swing alternately from left to right and back again, as loosely and freely as you can. Repeat this exercise 15–20 times.

03

04

01

DROPPING THE ARMS

Just like the previous exercise (see pp.42–3), this is a warm-up for the arms, the shoulders and the upper body as a whole. This deceptively simple exercise helps to move your chi outwards from its reservoir in your abdomen to your fingertips. The essence of this simple movement is the gentle swinging of your arms backwards and forwards, like a pendulum. You may begin to feel sensations in your palms and fingers, which are caused by the increased flow of chi .

(01) Stand with your back comfortably straight and your legs casually apart.

TIPS
• *Don't bend your fingers too much and don't swing your arms too far back, as this can create tension.*
• *Try not to drop or swing your arms too fast, but use only the minimum momentum required to complete the movement.*

02

(02) Raise both your arms in front so they are approximately horizontal, with the palms down. Your arms should not be rigidly straight; allow your elbows to bend slightly outwards and your arms to angle downwards. Keep your shoulders as relaxed as possible throughout.

03

(03) Drop your arms loosely. They should fall like a slack pendulum – shoulders acting as the pivot points. As your palms travel past and then behind your body, regain the momentum and swing as if you are trying to claw behind you. Try not to bend your fingers and don't swing your arms too far back as this can create tension. Return your arms to their initial horizontal position (see Step 02) and then drop them again; repeat 15–20 times.

Tai Chi beginning

The final movement of your morning routine is called Tai Chi Beginning and is the first movement in the Tai Chi form. Tai Chi ultimately aims to link individual exercises or movements into a single flowing sequence known as a 'form'. In all styles of Tai Chi the form begins with this movement, hence its name. But you can practise this move on its own if you need to calm yourself or improve your concentration. This exercise can also be a great confidence-builder for your regular Tai Chi practice.

02

(02) Turn your palms so that they face behind you.

01

(01) Stand comfortably with your feet shoulder-width apart, back straight and your arms hanging loosely, palms inwards. Keep your gaze forwards throughout the exercise.

03

04

(03) Raise your arms in front of you, keep a slight bend in your elbows and hold your fingers straight but relaxed. Here, your shoulders will act as a pivot.

(04) Draw your hands in about halfway towards your shoulders, keeping your palms down. Your elbows should point downwards rather than outwards.

Continued on next page

Tai Chi beginning

05

(05–06) Now, push down with your hands. Your elbows move and your shoulders act as a pivot. Your hands remain pointed slightly inwards as they trace a vertical path. As you push down bend your knees slightly as well.

(07) Return to the initial upright posture and repeat the entire movement 15 times.

06

07

CHAPTER THREE

Travelling with Tai Chi

Most people have a minimum of two journeys
a day – to and from work – and that's
10 journeys per week. The minutes and hours
spent travelling soon add up and can provide
an ideal opportunity for doing some Tai Chi.

With technological advances in transportation, the world has certainly become smaller, and faraway places are now far more accessible. Because of the ease and relative convenience of travel, we are choosing to travel longer distances, more frequently. But instead of reducing the amount of time travelling takes up in our day-to-day lives, nowadays we are choosing to spend more and more time commuting, whether this means making long daily train journeys, driving long distances or hopping on and off planes to conduct meetings abroad.

Unfortunately, with the exception of walking or cycling, most modes of travel involve time spent idly sitting, which is neither productive nor good for our health. But, you can convert this downtime into a health bonus by practising Tai Chi during your journey.

This chapter contains a variety of specially adapted Tai Chi exercises that can be performed while travelling, whether by car, plane, bus or train. These will help you maximise this travel time to improve your sense of well-being and ensure that you arrive at your destination relaxed, alert and untroubled by aches and pains.

These exercises have been designed to be feasible in the limited space available in most travelling situations. They are also relatively inconspicuous, to enable you to avoid unwelcome attention while you are performing them. To prepare yourself for doing Tai Chi on your journey, simply make sure you are wearing flat shoes.

Sinking the chest and plucking the back

This exercise is ideal to try while you are perhaps standing waiting in a queue or on a train, because the actual movement involved is very slight. It can be performed once or several times, depending on how much time you have available. It is regarded as one of the ten key exercises in Tai Chi by Yang Cheng-Fu in his famous work, *Yang's Ten Important Points*.

Although this exercise may appear to be mostly about breathing, its essence and objective is entirely different: the main focus is the coordinated movement of the chest, shoulders and back.

The traditional description of the movement The Sinking of the Chest and Plucking of the Back refers to the way in which your back forms an arc-like shape, and your chest becomes slightly collapsed. When you breathe in your head rises slightly, and as you exhale your head falls slightly, creating a slight nodding motion.

While this is an exercise for the upper part of your torso it also has a mental content as you visualise your back being plucked and pulled from behind while your shoulders are simultaneously drawn forwards and backwards. There is therefore a dual action, working in opposite directions, both physically and mentally. This encapsulates the philosophy of Tai Chi and is one of the reasons why this exercise is rightfully regarded as one of the vital movements of the art.

01

02

(01) Stand straight (or sit) and breathe in slowly and evenly. Inhale until your shoulders are slightly drawn back, with your chest protruding slightly. Allow your head to rise a little with the movement.

(02) Now breathe out, letting your head lower slightly with the movement. Allow your shoulders to move forwards and your back to curve outwards.

Wu Chi

In Chinese the term Wu Chi means 'the empty extreme' (this concept is discussed in more detail on page 20). The exercise named after this idea is fundamental to the art of Tai Chi. It is also known as the position of primal energy, which gives a clue as to its importance. If you perform it correctly, this posture can help you achieve a sense of deep relaxation while enabling you to access a vast resource of energy.

All the exercises in this book that begin with an upright posture start with an approximation of this Wu Chi stance, so it's well worth getting it right.

Unlike most Tai Chi exercises, Wu Chi entails an absence of apparent movement. It is more a posture than an exercise. You should always try to perform it in a way that is neutral and understated, so it's therefore an ideal posture to practise wherever you are – whether you are queuing to buy a ticket or standing on a packed bus or train. Since performing Wu Chi requires no more space than you need to stand in, you should be able to practise it even when you find yourself in a very crowded spot.

Your awareness of your sense of balance is heightened when you perform Wu Chi because it lowers your centre of gravity. You may be irritated by being buffeted about by the rough motion of a bus or train, but, in fact, a bumpy journey in which you have to stand provides an excellent opportunity to improve your balance by practising this important posture.

Stand with your feet shoulder-width apart. Place your left foot directly below your left shoulder and your right foot below your right shoulder. The outer edges of your feet should be parallel to one other.

Keep your back straight, but not stiff; you should feel a natural comfort and ease as you hold your body upright.

Allow your knees to bend slightly and your arms to hang loosely from your shoulders, with a little space for air in each armpit. Turn your palms inwards towards your centre and keep your fingers straight, relaxed and slightly apart.

TIPS
• Breathe slowly and evenly and let your inner body systems do their work.
• Try to develop a sense of your upper body being suspended from your head while your head is suspended from a golden thread.

- *Look straight ahead.*

- *Allow your chin to drop slightly.*

- *Allow your shoulders to drop slightly.*

- *Let your arms hang loosely and away from your sides.*

- *Relax your hips and belly so that neither bottom nor belly sticks out.*

- *Keep your fingers relaxed.*

- *Bend your knees slightly so they are not 'locked'.*

- *Make sure that the outer edges of your feet are parallel.*

Seated exercises

Despite the lack of space when you are sitting in a car, on a train or even on a plane, it is still possible to do some simple Tai Chi hand and foot exercises. These moves help to maintain healthy circulation and to prevent stiffness, particularly on long journeys.

These Tai Chi exercises can be performed unobtrusively from any comfortable sitting position. For the foot exercise, make sure that you are sitting properly with your feet flat on the floor initially – avoid crossing your legs or stretching them out.

Remember when doing even such simple exercises to do them consciously and carefully, but without tensing or straining any part of your body.

PALMS UP
(01) Sit straight and rest both of your hands comfortably on your thighs, with your palms uppermost.

(02) As you breathe in slowly, close your hands into fists, with moderate pressure, for a few seconds. As you exhale, relax and open your hands. Repeat this opening and closing movement 15–20 times.

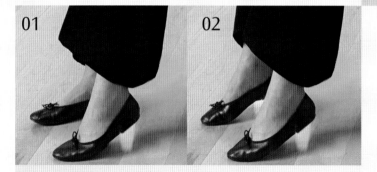

FOOT FLEXES
(01) Lift up the heel of your left foot, keeping your toes on the floor; return it to the ground slowly but firmly. Repeat this 15–20 times before doing the same on the right foot.

(02) Now, to finish, raise and lower the heels of both feet at the same time. Repeat this movement 15–20 times.

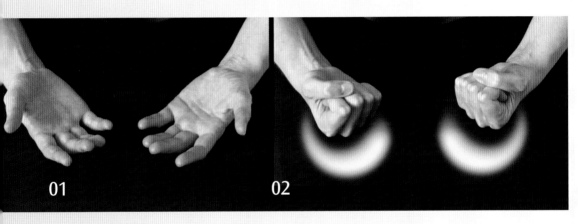

PALMS DOWN

(01) Hold your hands about 2 cm (1 in) above your thighs, with palms down. If you prefer, and have enough space, you can do this exercise with your hands beside your thighs. Your fingers should be straight but relaxed.

(02) As you breathe out, press forwards with the heels of your hands, flexing your wrists and raising your fingers upwards. As you breathe in, relax and draw your hands back slightly. Perform this exercise slowly but firmly 15–20 times.

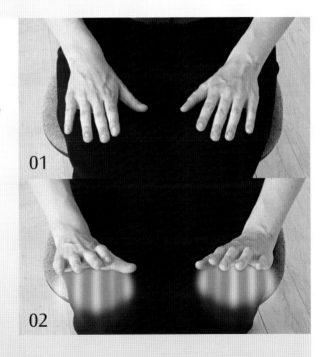

Walking

In health terms, walking is probably one of the few travelling methods worth complimenting. In the world of Chinese martial arts, the way you walk and manoeuvre your body is considered very important. Systems of walking are commonly known as steps in Chinese martial arts. Although there are many styles of steps in the Chinese martial arts our focus here is on the style of walking known as the Tai Chi Steps.

By practising this way of walking you can help to improve your sense of balance, which may prove invaluable in preventing strain and perhaps even injuries that can result from falls. Whenever you perform Tai Chi exercises with care and control, you are building muscle strength and coordination. What's more, you gain a mental advantage from focusing on your walking in this way: it can help improve your inner balance, which can in turn feed back into your internal chemistry, by reducing the damaging physiological effects of stress.

It's a good idea to get into the habit of practising Tai Chi Steps whenever you need to walk somewhere but are not in a hurry. Obviously, in the street, this would be a conspicuous way to walk, but a played-down version will still bring benefits if you get the chance to do it, even if you are holding a bag or have your hands in your pockets. The full version of Tai Chi Steps is great for boosting energy levels.

01

(01) Stand up straight with both hands resting on your hips. Let your arms hang wherever is comfortable, the focus here is on your legs. Put your feet together and bend your knees slightly. Transfer your weight to your right leg.

TIPS
- *Always keep your upper body as relaxed as possible.*
- *Hold your head level and look forwards.*

02   03   04

(02) *Extend your left foot with the toes pointing slightly outwards. Lower your left heel to the floor. Turn your upper body to face the same direction as your left foot, keeping your hips facing forwards.*

(03) *Now lower your left foot to the ground and transfer most of your weight forwards and down through your left leg. Keep your left knee bent.*

(04) *Because most of your weight is still on your left foot you can bring your right foot forward and place it next to your left. Place your right toes on the ground level with the left instep, your heel should be slightly elevated and both knees bent.*

Continued on next page

Walking

05   06

(05) *Keeping your left knee bent, extend your right foot, placing the heel on the ground, with the foot turned slightly outwards. As with the left foot, your right heel touches the ground, but the front of your foot is raised.*

(06) *Slowly and carefully lift your body forwards over the right leg as you lower your right toes to the ground.*

07 08

(07) Bring your left foot forward close to your right foot, keeping the heel slightly raised as before. You will notice that the movement takes a zig-zagging route.

(08) Then, turn your body slightly to the left and step forward moving your left foot in the same direction. From here, repeat the entire walking cycle, keeping the movement as smooth and flowing as possible.

CHAPTER FOUR

Tai Chi in the workplace

Work is a fact of life for most of us, but with a little imagination it is easy to customise your Tai Chi practice to fit in with your working day and you will soon feel the benefit.

Work has been an integral part of daily lives since pre-historic times, when our ancestors hunted for food or cultivated crops. Our careers and jobs today are simply sophisticated versions of those primitive duties and responsibilities. Work in all its forms dominates our lives, both in terms of the time it occupies and in terms of the importance we assign to it.

There are hundreds of different occupations and the variety of working conditions is equally vast. Some people work in open-plan offices that lack any privacy, while others work in enclosed and suffocating environments. Some do physical work outside all day while others sit indoors most of the time.

Given that working consumes so much of our time, it is desirable to try to do some Tai Chi during the working day. This chapter will show you how this is possible. Ideally you will practise all the exercises described on most days of the week, but if this is not feasible select and customise the exercises to your individual situation. Choose those that are the most appropriate and suited to your particular working environment. If you have privacy, do the conspicuous exercises; if not, do the more subtle ones. Any Tai Chi practice you manage to include in your working day will be of benefit to your effectiveness and sense of well-being.

Diagonal flight

When you bend your body forwards and compress your chest for a long time, such as when you are hunched over your desk working, you will feel like having a good stretch from time to time – extending your arms to open up your chest – it's the 'classic' stretching movement. However, in taking this compensatory action, there is a risk that you may overstretch yourself and this can be damaging. It may feel good at first, but such drastic stretching is not always the best thing you can do.

Originally a standing gesture, the Tai Chi movement known as Diagonal Flight involves a moderate widening of both arms and opening up of the chest, and it is a good substitute for uncontrolled overstretching. This movement has been adapted as a sitting exercise for this book and is ideal if you are an office worker who spends a good part of the day sitting at a desk to write or using the computer. Try it out whenever you feel the need for a good stretch.

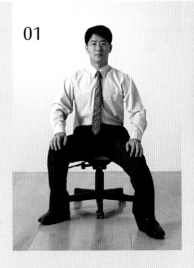

01

(01) Sit comfortably and upright on your chair and rest both hands on your knees. Move your left foot forwards, turning it slightly outwards. Bring your right leg back and turn it slightly outwards too.

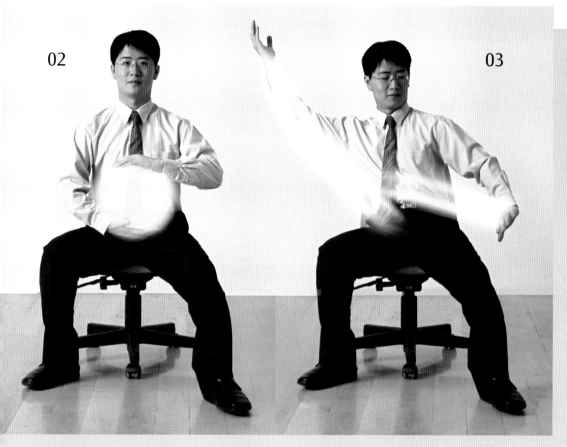

02

03

(02) *Bring your hands to the position known as Holding the Ball. Place your right hand under the 'ball' and let your left hand rest on its top.*

(03) *Now spread your arms. Your right hand curves outwards and upwards. Simultaneously, your left hand curves outwards and downwards until parallel with your left leg. The nature of the movement is a gentle 'half-spiralling' arc. As you move your arms out, lean back slightly and face the right. Hold this posture for a few seconds before curving your hands back to the Holding the Ball posture. Repeat 15 times.*

Continued on next page

Diagonal flight

04

05

(04–06)
Now repeat, placing
your right foot forwards
and outwards and your
left foot slightly back
and facing outwards.
Place your left hand
below when holding the
'ball'. Curve your right
arm outwards and
downwards and your
left arm outwards and
upwards.

Repeat 15 times on this
side.

06

Wild horse parts its mane

This exercise is closely connected with Diagonal Flight (pp. 64–7). Similarly this is a sitting adaptation of an original standing posture. Wild Horse Parts Its Mane is also suitable for stretching the arms after a long period of sedentary work.

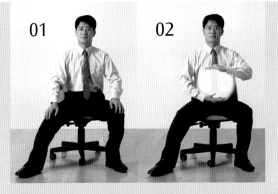

(01) Begin by sitting upright with your legs positioned as in Step 04, page 66.

(02) Bring your hands together to the Holding the Ball position, your left hand resting on the top of the 'ball' and your right hand supporting it from below.

(03–04) Now spread your arms, moving your right hand outwards and upwards in a clockwise 'half-spiral' movement until it is approximately level, palm facing inwards, towards your head. At the same time move your left arm downwards and outwards in a clockwise 'half-spiral' until your arm is almost straight and your hand is downwards. As you move your arms, lean your body diagonally forwards and to the right, turning your head to gaze out beyond your right palm.

03   04

As you complete the stretch, your arms should be almost straight, with your elbows relaxed. Hold this stretch briefly before returning to Holding the Ball position. Remember that your right hand is underneath. When you draw your hands together, they should move along an arc rather than a 'half-spiral' path. Repeat this exercise 15 times.

Now perform this stretch on the other side. This time, your left foot should be placed forward; your left arm spirals diagonally forwards and your right arm backwards. When holding the 'ball', your left hand is below and your right hand above.

Tai Chi beginning ~ sitting

This exercise is simply the sitting adaptation of the exercise introduced on pages 46–9, one of the most familiar movements of Tai Chi. If you carry it out during your working day it can help to calm your mind and allow you to focus better.

01

(01) Sit squarely on your chair, with your arms hanging loosely at your sides, palms face inwards.

(02–03) With relaxed arms raise your hands slowly in front of you, palms facing downwards. Your fingers should be straight and slightly separated. Keeping your shoulders relaxed, continue to raise your arms until your hands are level with your shoulders.

(04) Now draw your hands towards you, allowing your elbows to drop towards the floor. Stop when your hands are near to your shoulders.

(05) Then lower your arms by pressing your hands downwards until you reach the starting position, with your arms by your sides. Try to keep your palms facing downwards for as long as practical throughout this downwards movement. Relax your wrists and let your hands drop loosely. Repeat 15 times.

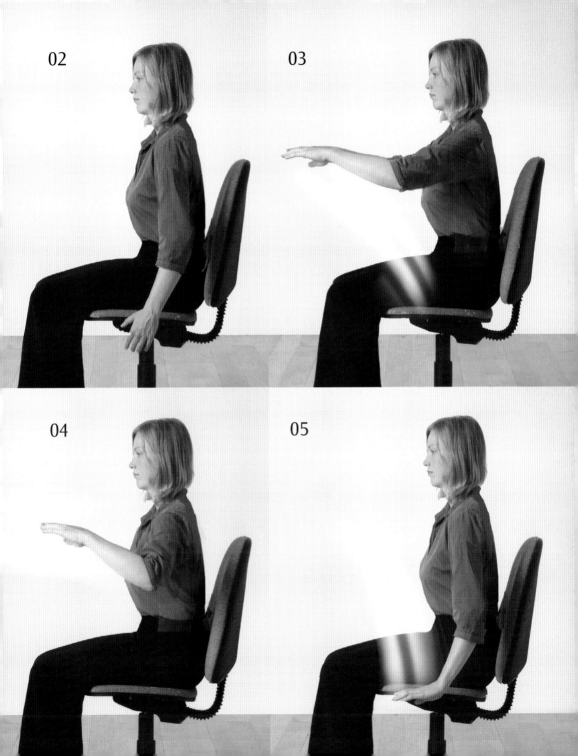

Golden rooster stands on one leg ~ standing

This exercise is a modified version of a well-known Tai Chi movement of the same name. The original may be too conspicuous to carry out in the workplace so this version has been specially adapted for practising while you are at work.

Golden Rooster is particularly useful for building leg strength and improving your sense of balance. In Tai Chi physical balance and internal balance – both internal organs and the mind – are inseparable. Practising this movement, therefore, can help enhance your physical coordination, regulate your internal chemistry and promote psychological equilibrium.

You will need to find yourself a chair, desk or cabinet that stands at about waist height for support. If this is not possible try using a wall. Change into flat shoes or simply remove them altogether. You will find a further adaptation, which is performed sitting down, on page 74.

01

(01) Stand upright and use your chosen support, positioned on your right side, to find balance. Relax and breathe naturally from your belly.

02   **03**

(02) *Slowly, bending your elbow, raise the front of your left wrist. Keep your wrist relaxed and your fingers hanging straight and angled slightly downwards. Imagine that there is a string connecting your hand to your knee – as your hand rises your knee follows. The thigh muscles are contracted, but the rest of your leg and your foot are relaxed, dangling loosely.*

(03) *When your hand reaches shoulder height, flex both your hand and your foot so that they are pointing upwards. Freeze the movement. After a short pause, slowly return to the starting position.*
  Repeat 15 times and then do the exercise raising your right arm and leg.

Golden rooster stands on one leg ~ sitting

This exercise has the same origins as the modified standing exercise on the previous pages and will help you to concentrate on and improve your sense of balance. The focus here is on the coordination of the moving arm and leg. It may seem less demanding than the standing version, but it still requires your full focus in order to perform it correctly.

01

(01) Sit with your legs slightly apart, your back upright and your palms resting on your knees.

Visualisation
Imagine you are a puppeteer – there is a string tied between your hand and your knee. When your hand is on your knee, the string is slack. As the hand rises, the string becomes taut and pulls your knee upwards.

02

03

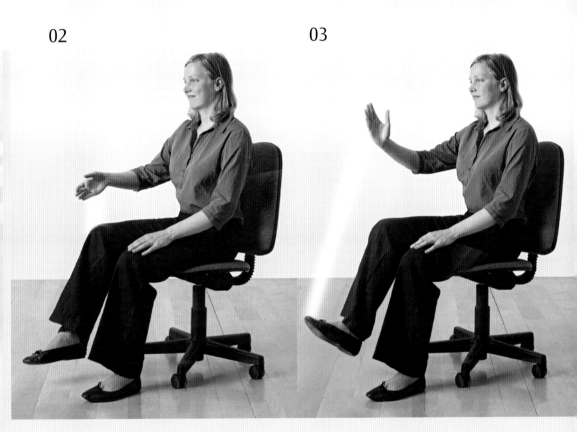

(02) *Lift your right forearm so that your hand is directly above your right knee and your palm facing the left. Your wrist is completely relaxed and your hand angled downwards. Your fingers are relaxed, but straight. As you raise your arm in a smooth movement, your right thigh follows. There is no strength or tension in your calf, ankle or foot; they dangle freely.*

(03) *The distance between your hand and your knee should be constant.*

As your hand reaches shoulder height, stop the upward movement and flex your wrist and foot. Now, slowly return your foot to the floor and your hand to your knee. The entire movement should be slow, smooth and even. Repeat 15 times with your right leg and 15 times with your left.

Chi – press in

This movement is known as 'Chi' in Chinese, which in this context means 'to squeeze' or 'to compress'. For this exercise you will need to stand in front of a solid wall that is clear of any pictures or other distractions. Be aware that some office walls are merely screens or partitions and are not strong enough to use in this exercise. Do not attempt to perform against a glass wall or window.

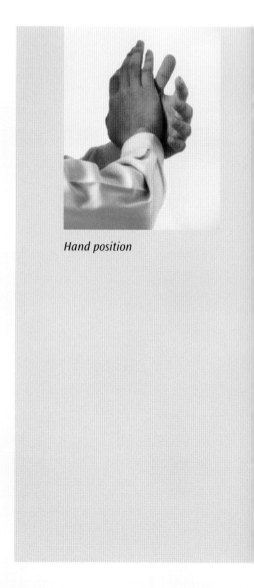

Hand position

01

(01) Stand facing the wall at a distance of about 60 cm (2 ft). The precise distance depends on your height, so you may want to adjust it when you have tried the exercise.

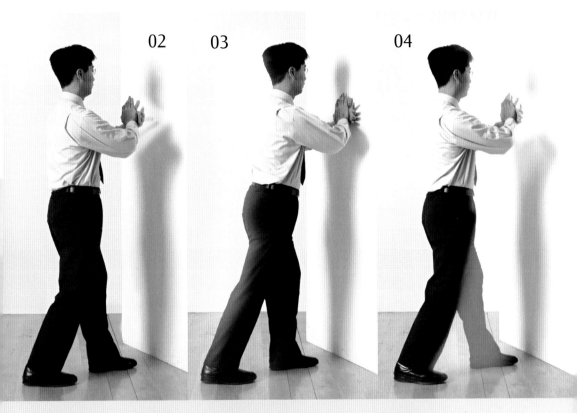

02 **03** **04**

(02) Bend both knees slightly and step forwards with your left foot. Clasp your palms together in front of your chest with the right palm facing outwards and the left palm facing inwards (see detail photograph left).

(03) Slowly straighten your right leg and lean your body slightly forwards as you slowly press your hands onto the wall. The force you exert should be firm and smooth.

(04) Allow the recoil of your own force to bounce you back from the wall.

Repeat this exercise 15–20 times. Then reverse hand and leg positions and perform the exercise a further 15–20 times.

An – push out

Push Out – 'An' in Chinese – is a gesture which signifies one of the four cardinal points. As with the previous exercise, stand in front of a clear wall at a distance of about 60 cm (2 ft).

Do not think of this exercise simply as pushing into the wall. Instead, visualise trying to reach out beyond the wall, but being interrupted by the presence of the wall. The slight straightening of the arms should not stop because your hands touch the wall; their movement should be smooth, uniform and uninterrupted by contact with the wall.

01

(01) Stand in Wu Chi, facing the wall

VARIATION

If you are unable to exercise against a wall or some other solid structure, you can use an imaginary wall.

Stretch out into midair and straighten your arms as before when pushing. When you withdraw your arms transfer your weight onto your back foot. Turn your hands inwards slightly, and then stretch out again.

02
03
04

(02) Relax both knees and step forwards with your left foot, allowing your weight to sink back onto the right foot. Raise both hands in front of your chest, about shoulder-width apart, with your palms facing diagonally downwards and your elbows angled outwards. Keep your upper body upright.

(03) Straighten your right leg and lean your body slightly forwards towards the wall, straightening your arms slightly.

(04) Push out slowly and gently against the wall continuing to straighten your arms. As you make contact, let your own force propel you backwards.

Repeat the movement 15 times. Now perform the exercise with your right foot forwards.

Peng & Lu – ward off and roll back

This exercise is an adaptation of two sequences of movement known in Ancient China as Peng and Lu. These form part of the full Tai Chi form.

The movements of this exercise are flowing and rounded and it is important to bear this in mind while you practise them.

This exercise represents the remaining two cardinal directions.

(02) Raise both hands so that they are level with your abdomen, palms facing inwards, shoulder-width apart. Allow your elbows to bend softly, and keep your hands a comfortable distance from your body – neither too near nor too far.

(01) Begin by standing in Wu Chi.

03

04

(03) Turn your body towards the right approximately 45°. Shift your weight slightly. Using your right heel as a pivot, turn your foot outwards. Using the ball of your left foot as a pivot turn your foot slightly towards the right. Your head, upper body and your right foot should now be aligned.

As you turn, swing both arms slightly outwards and upwards. Along with the movement caused by your turning body, this slight swing causes the hands to travel in a smooth arcing gesture. When your right hand reaches shoulder height, the back of your hand is aligned in front of your body, palm facing inwards. The left palm faces diagonally downwards.

(04) Change the direction of the palms by turning both hands anti-clockwise. The palm of your right hand now faces outwards and your left palm faces diagonally upwards.

Continued on next page

Peng & Lu – ward off and roll back

05

06

(05) *Lower both hands to the level of your hips, maintaining their position relative to each other. At the same time shift your weight back onto your left foot.*

(06) *Turn both hands again so that the left palm faces down and the right faces up. Keep your gaze and head facing the same direction as your right hand.*

07

08

(07) *Now move both hands in an arc upwards and forwards until the right arm is moderately straight with the palm facing inwards, and the left palm is facing diagonally downwards. Shift your weight slightly forwards onto your right foot.*

(08) *Turn your hands once more and repeat the sequence 15 times from Step 04. The whole motion should be smooth but deliberate. Now return to Step 01 and repeat with the arm and leg positions reversed.*

Single whip

In its classic form this is a challenging Tai Chi movement that requires strength and control. It is shown here in a modified form that is within the capability of most Tai Chi practitioners. To gain the full benefit of this sequence, you will need to concentrate on performing the movement with care, paying attention to the detail.

NOTE
This exercise is a little more demanding, in terms of co-ordination, than some of the others in this book. Do not over-correct yourself while you are practising and try to do the entire sequence in one smooth motion. In time, and with some practice, you will easily master its subtlety.

(01) Begin by standing in Wu Chi.

(02) Lower yourself by bending your knees slightly. At the same time raise both hands in front of you so they are approximately level with your face, palms facing upwards. Your fingers should be touching, straight, but relaxed. Keep your elbows dropped.

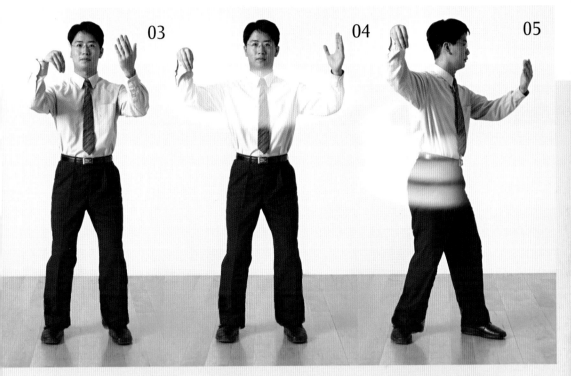

(03) Draw the thumb and fingertips of your right hand down together to form a point, keeping your fingers straight. This beak-like shape is described as a 'hook'. Point the hook downwards.

(04) Move your elbows apart to widen the space between your hands. Your hands will appear to have turned, but the only real movement is in your shoulder joints.

(05) Turn to face the left by twisting at the waist and turning both feet. Now swivel on your left heel, swinging your toes back round to face left. Keeping your right toes on the floor, swivel your right heel outwards to the right. Your right arm with the hook remains in position relative to your body and therefore appears to swing towards the left as you turn. Your left hand moves slightly downwards but does not turn with your body – your palm should face inwards.

Continued on next page

Single whip

(06–07) Now turn your left palm out and straighten your arm very slightly, pushing forwards from your right leg. As you glide forwards your weight is transferred to your left leg. Your right hand remains in position with its hook facing downwards, but the arm straightens slightly as your body moves forwards and away from your hand.

08

09

(08) Now bring both arms together and turn your body and feet to face forwards once again. This returns you to the earlier position 02 (see p.84).

(09) Now form a hook with your left hand and perform the movement sequence on the other side.

Repeat this sequence on both sides 15 times.

Play the lute

The literal translation of the name of this exercise is 'Hands Strumming the Pipa'. The pipa is a form of Chinese plucked string instrument, sometimes called a Chinese lute, which dates back to the 2nd century BCE to the Qin Dynasty. It is sometimes regarded as the king of Chinese instruments.

Unlike Western guitars and lutes, which are often held horizontally and plucked, pipa are typically held vertically in the lap. The name of this Tai Chi movement therefore describes the hand gestures used when playing the pipa. To the Western mind, a more suitable description might be playing the lute.

01

(01) Stand in Wu Chi. Make sure you are fully relaxed. Your arms hang loosely from your shoulders and your hands hang loosely with your palms naturally facing inwards towards your thighs.

(02) Mentally check your body and allow each muscle to relax. Breathe naturally and slowly raise your hands, palms inwards, in front of you. When both hands are at approximately the same level as your belly, switch their relative position by rolling your hands inwards along the path of a circle. The left hand therefore becomes higher and further out than your right.

(03) When your left hand is at the same height as your shoulder, flip both hands up by flexing your wrists. At the same time, sink your weight by bending your right leg slightly and flex your left foot, resting your left heel on the floor.

Return to the initial standing position and repeat the sequence 15 times. Then perform the exercise with the positions of the hands and feet reversed. If you wish you may alternate sides.

02

03

White crane flaunts wings

This is a literal translation of the Chinese name for this exercise and it will help your practice if you can visualise this bird's graceful movements.

Once your arms are fully spread, return to the initial standing position. Repeat the entire sequence 15 times and then perform the mirror version 15 times too. In the mirror version, your left leg is extended forwards and when holding the imaginary ball, your left hand is above your right.

It may be confusing at first knowing which arm rises up and which one descends when you are spreading your arms. Just remember that the extended leg is on the same side as the descending arm. For those who are more sensitive, the unfavourable changes in balance will tell you when you are doing this incorrectly.

(02–03) Bring your hands together to hold the ball, your left hand is underneath and your right hand on top. At the same time, extend your right foot in front of you and swivel your left foot out to point to the left. Your feet should be approximately shoulder-width apart and your weight evenly spread. Your knees are in line with, but not poking beyond, your toes. Bring your palms together to collapse the ball. Keep most of your weight on your left leg and lean forwards from the hip, bending your left knee as you do so. As you lean forwards, keep your arms softly curved and bring the collapsed ball down to rest on your right knee.

01

(01) Stand in Wu Chi and make sure that you are thoroughly relaxed. Breathe naturally from the belly.

02

03

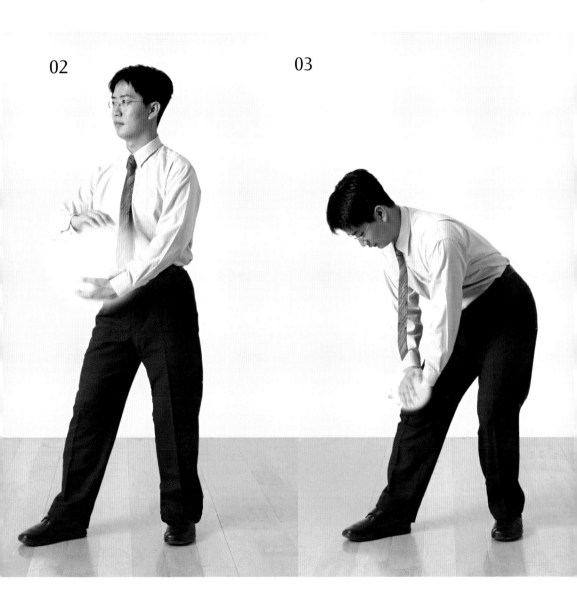

Continued on next page

White crane flaunts wings

(04–05) Now lean back and straighten your body again while spreading your arms out. Your left arm curves diagonally upwards and your right arm downwards and outwards. Your left palm still faces upwards and inwards, and your right palm downwards. Finally as you reach the full stretch, flip your left hand to face outwards and pull up the toes of your left foot (not shown).

(06) Lift the toes of your right foot. Keep your weight mostly on your left foot; the heel of your right foot is simply maintaining your balance. Continue moving your left hand diagonally upwards and your right hand moving outwards.

Slowly and calmly return to Wu Chi. Repeat this sequence 15 times and then reverse hand and feet positions and repeat a further 15 times.

04

05

06

Unwinding with Tai Chi

Practise these gentle, restorative exercises as soon as you return home after work, or later in the evening, to help refresh you and prepare you for sleep.

Many of us are working harder than ever before – holding down more than one job, perhaps, or carrying out a variety of roles in life, paid and unpaid. And the way we organise our lives often increases physical and mental strain. Evening activities play a greater part than those of our forebears, whose evenings seem to have been simpler. People returned from work, ate, rested and went to bed early. Nowadays we use our free time to the full, spending evenings with colleagues and friends, socialising in bars, restaurants and clubs, at the cinema and theatre, or even playing sports and going to the gym. Whether we do this for fun, as part of work, for education or self-improvement, all such activities place a strain on the body and/or mind. We have less time to refresh ourselves after a busy day and may suffer from poor sleep patterns as a result. Some people do try to relax in the evening, perhaps in front of the television, but this is not true relaxation since the mind is engaged, while the body is inactive. What is often missing is the kind of exercise that is de-stressing for both mind and body.

The exercises in this chapter will help you to unwind and actively relax your body and mind after a busy day. Change into some comfortable clothes and practise these movements whenever it best suits you – when you get home, before dinner or just before bedtime. The exercises are neither strenuous nor demanding – the aim being to make your evenings more peaceful than your days.

Sweeping side to side

This exercise is one of those fundamental movements to many of the Chinese martial arts. This movement is particularly useful for loosening the shoulders at the end of the day, when they may be stiff from sitting at a desk or tense as a result of more generalised workplace stress. The key to this exercise is getting the hang of relaxing your shoulders while at the same time maintaining stability in your torso and legs.

Relax and let your arms swing to the left and right. One swing does not have to immediately follow on after the other – when your arms are raised, you can pause slightly before you start on the next swing.

It is best to breathe in when your arms are up and breathe out as you sweep your arms down and across.

Some people have a tendency to 'bounce' while performing this exercise – you can avoid this by making sure that your stance is slightly lowered, knees bent and weight sunk right down. Feel that your legs are heavy and 'glued' to the floor – this will help you keep them perfectly still while you move your upper body.

01

(01) Stand in Wu Chi, breathe slowly and naturally from your belly. Take a few minutes to check over your whole body and make sure it is completely relaxed.

02

(02) Raise both hands to your right. Your left hand should end up at the same level as your shoulders, and your right hand should end up level with your head. Keep your shoulders relaxed, your arms slightly bent at the elbow, your fingers relaxed and lightly curled in – imagine you are holding an egg in each hand.

03

(03) Swing both hands down and bring them up again on your left side. Let your arms sweep in front of you – swinging your whole arm, not just your forearms. This is a rapid movement, but speed is not a priority. Just use enough momentum to swing your arms loosely and comfortably. Keep your shoulders relaxed and your head facing forwards.

Drag hands

Despite its name, the emphasis of this exercise is not on the hands, but further down the body. It exercises your waist more than any other part.

In the literary tradition of Tai Chi the waist carries the same degree of importance as the key ideas and concepts discussed in Chapter One (see pp.12–29). In Tai Chi practice the waist is one of the most vital parts of the body. There are many traditional metaphors describing its importance: the controller of motion, an army banner, an axle, while the *chi* is the wheel. In other words, the waist directs and stabilises the energy that flows through your body.

(02) Sweep both hands to your right in a circular movement in front of you, until they are at approximately shoulder height. Your left arm will be bent and your right arm almost straight. Keep your fingers straight but relaxed.

(03) Turn your waist slowly but firmly in an anti-clockwise direction. This movement drags your hands towards the left. Remember that the movement of your hands is secondary to the turning of your waist.

01

(01) Stand with your back straight and your legs apart, bent slightly at the knees. Position your feet so that the distance between them is wider than shoulder-width, but not uncomfortably so. Allow both arms to hang comfortably away from your sides.

02

03

Continued on next page

Drag hands

Sink your weight low so that you have a firm base. Because you are adopting a wider stance you should take care to keep your knees in line with, but not protruding over, your toes. This open stance is rather like sitting astride an invisible horse.

With your weight fully sunk, feel that your spine is lengthened, your bottom is just hanging, not sticking out or pulled in, the top of your body is light, your shoulders relaxed and your head is suspended by a golden thread. Because of this lengthening of your spine you feel free to rotate the upper half of your body slowly, gently, and smoothly to the left and the right. Do not strain or overstretch, but remain relaxed.

(04) As your hands complete the movement to the left, your right arm will be bent and your left arm relatively straight. Now flip both hands over so that the palms face forwards again.

(05) Turn from your waist, this time towards the right. Your arms again sweep across as they are dragged by the turning of your waist. Keep your hands at the same height as they sweep across.

Repeat the sequence 15–20 times.

04

05

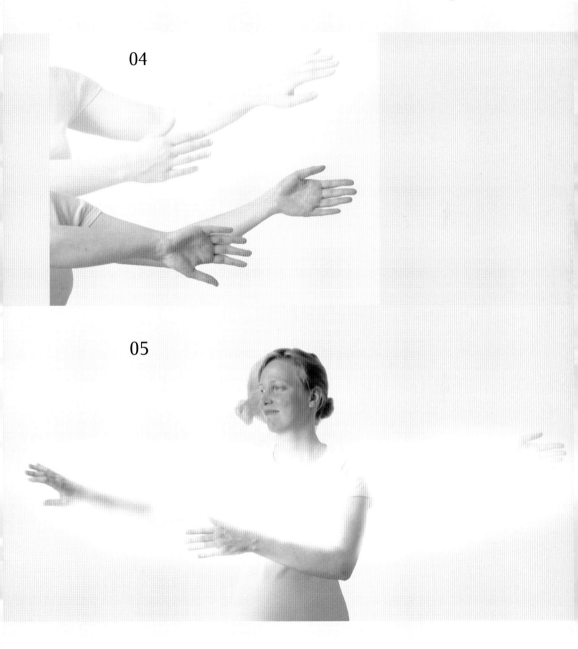

Carry the tiger and return to the mountain

Despite its colourful title, this name is simply a visual allusion to the gesture of carrying something bulky, as you'll see in the second half of this movement (see pages 103–4). The steps in the first part of this sequence allude to the standing exercise on page 40, which is commonly referred to as Cross Hands.

Use this exercise at the end of your working day, both to restore your inner tranquillity and to recharge your batteries for the evening's activities.

01

(01) Stand in Wu Chi.

NOTE
Throughout the movement, keep your head facing forwards, your fingers straight but soft. Your arms should always remain relaxed and slightly bent. Try to keep your shoulders dropped and relaxed.
Repeat this sequence 15–20 times.

(02) Slowly draw your hands up and cross them in front of your chest; your left hand should be under your right hand and both palms face upwards.

(03) Continue to raise your hands upwards. As they pass in front of your face flip both hands over so that the palms now face outwards, but remain crossed.

(04) Now move your hands outwards, tracing a circular path, your palms turning to face out to the sides with your arms relatively straight.

Continued on next page

Carry the tiger and return to the mountain

05   **06**

(05) Now start to circle both arms down. Slowly bending your legs, keeping your back straight and imagine your weight sinking right down through the floor.

(06) As your arms sweep down to the floor, you reach the lowest posture in the sequence. Slowly continue the circular sweeps of your arms, bringing your hands together until they are a shoulder-width apart.

(07) *As you start straightening your legs and rising up again, turn your palms to face upwards and raise your forearms as though you are carrying a very heavy object.*

(08) *When your legs are almost straight and your hands reach chest level, cross them with your left hand underneath.*

Repeat the entire cycle of circling the arms and carrying the tiger.

Dead float

The literal translation from Chinese for this position is Lying Like a Corpse. It is a breathing exercise especially designed for relaxing both your mind and your body and is therefore ideal for practising in bed just before you fall asleep. If you have trouble sleeping you may find this exercise particularly helpful. It may also help, if you suffer from chronic insomnia, to give some attention to your sleeping environment.

The Chinese art of Feng Shui teaches us that for optimum relaxation and beneficial sleep, your bedroom should be not be cluttered with extraneous objects that create distraction and visual 'noise'. Also, colours in the bedroom should be tranquil and harmonious.

As you relax in this position, remember the eight key words for breathing that have been passed down from ancient times:

Soft – Even – Small – Slow – Deep – Gentle – Continuous – Long

Rest your head comfortably on your pillow, neither too high nor too low, to avoid any neck strain. Don't lie on your side, but flat on your back with your legs falling outwards in a natural and relaxed way. Rest your arms comfortably, away from your sides with your palms facing downwards.

Close your eyes, empty your mind of any thoughts, and breathe gently. Breathe in and out slowly and evenly, allowing you to slowly fall asleep at the end of your busy day.

CHAPTER SIX

Extended practice

When you have a little more time to devote to your Tai Chi practice, try the following sequences that join many of the movements you have already learned into a graceful and satisfying whole.

In its purest form Tai Chi is a sequence of linked movements that gently stretch and strengthen the body and relax and focus the mind. However, the main part of this book has been aimed at helping you fit individual Tai Chi elements into your busy life. While it is beyond the scope of this book to fully describe and teach the entire sequence of Tai Chi, most readers will be interested in learning how to advance their practice. In this chapter you will be shown how some of the exercises in the previous chapters can be linked in a flowing Tai Chi form.

There are three sequences for you to practise when you have time for a longer-than-usual session – perhaps at a weekend or when you are on holiday. Make such a practice session an opportunity to create a period of undisturbed tranquillity. Choose a time when you will not be interrupted by the telephone or other external communications so that you can study the movements carefully and concentrate on performing them as accurately as possible.

Although each sequence should be regarded as a single movement, you will soon recognise elements you have learnt in earlier chapters. Inevitably when you first try these longer sequences you will find that you stop and start as you struggle to remember the precise movements required. But you should be constantly mindful of the unity of the sequence and attempt to perform it as smoothly as you can without overcorrecting yourself.

Lazily tighten the clothes/1

This set of movements is often considered as one gesture under the name Lazily Tighten the Clothes. Its alternative name – Peng Lu Chi An – reflects that this series of movements is composed of four individual gestures, each with a one-character title (see Chapter Four for individual movements).

Lazily Tighten the Clothes is a sequence found in all forms and styles of Tai Chi, and is one of the cornerstones of the art. You start in the Wu Chi posture (see page 54) and then you slowly raise your hands. You then turn to your right, swinging out both arms and twisting your legs. Next, you flip both hands and drag them down towards your belly (this is the Peng and Lu exercises as explained on pages 80–3). In the next phase of the sequence you lift up your left hand to around shoulder level and bring your right hand to the left, crossing over your right hand.

Then, you turn your arms and upper body back to the right and press your crossed hands forwards; this is the Chi or Press In gesture (see pages 76–7).

You then turn your hands palms down and separate them by a shoulder-width. You draw your weight back, so that your arms are also pulled back and down to chest level. Finally, you push your arms forwards, completing the sequence with the An or Push Out movement (see pages 78–9).

(01) *Begin in the Wu Chi pose. Mentally check your whole body and allow each muscle to relax. Breathe slowly and naturally.*

(02) *Slowly raise your hands to chest level, Your palms are facing each other – imagine that they are resting against the sides of a glowing ball of energy.*

(03) *Lift the toes of your right foot and swivel on your heel so that your foot is pointed towards the right, then lower your toes. At the same time gently turn your hips; your body will follow. Raise your hands and, keeping them in the same lightly curved shape, lift and swing them out slightly to the right.*

03

Continued on next page

Lazily tighten the clothes/2

04

(04) Now, smoothly flip both hands over towards the left. Your right palm is now facing out and your left palm is uppermost.

(05–06) Slowly transfer your weight down through your left leg, as you turn slightly at the waist, drawing your hands down towards your belly. Follow this movement with your gaze.

05

06

Continued on next page

Lazily tighten the clothes/3

(07–08) Turning slightly at the waist, swing your left hand upwards and outwards; keep your focus on your left palm. Try to feel that there is an energetic connection between the palms of your hands.

07

(09) Now, turn your left palm to face outwards as you draw your right palm up to rest against it. Your crossed palms press lightly outwards.

08

09

Continued on next page

Lazily tighten the clothes/4

(10) Twist from the waist so that you are now facing to the right. Your hands and arms remain crossed in front of your chin.

10

11

12

(11) Shift most of your weight down through your right leg. Your arms and torso will naturally move forwards as you do so. Now, press forwards lightly with your crossed hands.

(12) Slide your left hand over your right as you turn your right palm down.

Continued on next page

Lazily tighten the clothes/5

13

(13) Separate your hands and glide them outwards until they are in line with your shoulders. Your arms should remain softly curved and relaxed at the elbows.

(14–15) Slowly transfer your weight on to your left (back) leg, and as you do so draw your elbows down and back slightly until your hands are at chest level. As your body moves backwards, lift the toes of your right foot. Now most of your weight is on your left leg; your right heel acts as a stabiliser.

14

15

Continued on next page

Lazily tighten the clothes/6

(16–17) In the final phase, transfer your weight forwards onto your right leg and gently but firmly push your hands upwards and outwards. You don't need to raise your hands too high, just try to keep your palms in line with your shoulders.

This An or Push Out movement completes the whole sequence, thus concluding Lazily Tighten the Clothes.

16

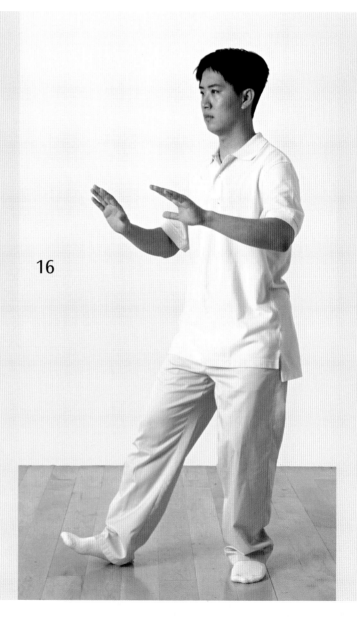

17

Drag hands and single whip/1

This sequence of Tai Chi movements is distinctive and combines two movements: Single Whip shown in Chapter Four (see pages 84–7) and Drag Hands shown in Chapter Five (see pages 98–101). Before you start the sequence make sure you feel confident with its individual components.

You start off with your legs together and knees bent. You extend your right arm and form a 'hook' with your right hand.

After turning to the left, you go on to flip your left hand so that the palm is outermost and pressed forwards (this is the left-side Single Whip movement). You glide your weight forwards, bringing your right arm with its hooked hand to your left (this posture is similar to the An or Push Out exercise (see page 78–9).

Now, you flip your hands sideways and drag them across to the right, turning your waist as you do so (this is the Drag Hands movement). Your left hand now becomes a hook and you draw it back and transfer your weight on to your left leg.

Finally, you bring your right arm and leg back to the centre and, turning towards the right, you press your right hand forwards in another Single Whip gesture.

Throughout this sequence, the movements of your shoulders and back are subtle and delicate.

(01) Stand with your feet together and knees bent. Extend your right arm out to the side, forming a hook with your right hand. Hold your left hand in front of your body at chin level. Sink your entire weight down through your right leg and lift your left heel off the ground.

(02) Turn your body to the left and swing your left leg out in an arc as you do so. Then, bring the heel to rest at a right angle to your right foot more than a shoulder-width away. Maintain your arm position, moving only with the twist of your torso.

01

02

Continued on next page

Drag hands and single whip/2

03

(03–04) Lower your toes and transfer most of your weight down through your left leg. As you do this turn your left palm outwards and push it forwards. This step is the left-side Single Whip movement.

04

Continued on next page

Drag hands and single whip/3

(05) Now, with most of your weight already forwards, lose the hook and swing your right arm forwards to join with your left in a slight forwards push. This posture resembles the An or Push Out exercise.

(06–07) Turn your upper body to face the front, swivel on your right heel and turn your right foot to the right and turning your hands anti-clockwise. Notice how your right hand is pulled across the chest by the move. Keep your left hand stretched out to your left.

05

06

07

Continued on next page

Drag hands and single whip/4

08

(08) Turn from the waist and allow the movement to sweep both arms towards the right. This is the movement of Drag Hands.

(09–11) Flex your right hand up and draw your left wrist up above your head, forming a hook with your thumb and fingers. Centre your weight through both legs.

Continued on next page

Drag hands and single whip/5

(12) Transfer all of your weight down through your left leg and swing the hook out to the left.

(13) Imagine that your right hand and right leg are connected and that your hand is lifting your foot and pulling it inwards. Rest your right toes beside your left foot and, at the same time, bring your hand across and in front of your chest.

12

13

Continued on next page

Drag hands and single whip/6

14

15

(14–15) Keeping all your weight down through your left leg, turn from the waist and swing your right arm and right leg out to the right, bringing your heel to rest more than a shoulder-width out from your left foot.

(16) Lower your right toes, transferring your weight back to the centre. Flip your right hand so that the palm faces out and press forward. This is the final movement of the sequence – another Single Whip gesture, but this time the direction is to the right.

16

Finishing sequence/1

Unlike Lazily Tighten the Clothes (see pages 110–121), this series of movements does not bear a unique name. But it does combine movements shown in previous chapters – Cross Hands (see pages 40–1) and Carry the Tiger and Return to the Mountain (see pages 102–5) with a sequence known as Tai Chi Ending that is introduced here for the first time. This resembles Tai Chi Beginning (see pages 46–9) and always marks the end of a Tai Chi session. This entire movement is a great example of how the exercises shown in previous chapters can be joined in the Tai Chi form and makes a fitting ending to this book and any Tai Chi session.

You start this sequence from the Wu Chi pose (see pages 54–5). First, you raise your hands and cross them in front of your chest at shoulder height. You continue to raise and straighten your arms and as they reach the top, you turn the palms outwards. Then, you sweep your arms down and bend your legs to lower your body before bringing your hands forwards and up as your legs straighten (this is Carry the Tiger and Return to the Mountain).

Once your legs are almost straight and your hands are at hip level, you turn both hands down. The sequence ends by pushing the hands vertically downwards and returning to Wu Chi.

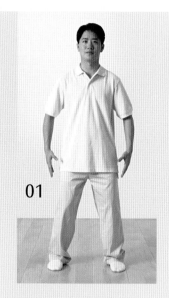

01

(01) Stand in Wu Chi. Mentally check your whole body and try to relax any muscle tension you detect. Breathe deeply, slowly and naturally from your belly.

(02) Slowly raise both hands, crossing your wrists at shoulder height. Make sure that there is still a little space in each armpit.

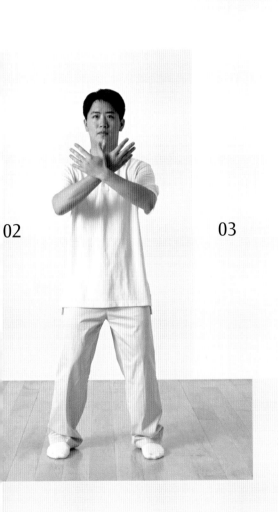

02

03

(03) Continue to raise your arms upwards, flipping both hands over as they pass in front of your face so that your palms face out.

Continued on next page

Finishing sequence/2

(04) Continue to raise your hands up and over your head and then outwards to each side. As your hands reach the top of the arc, turn your palms outwards.

(05) Slowly spread your arms, continuing this wide circular movement. As you start to bring your arms down, mirror this downwards movement by slowly lowering your stance. You can bend at both the knee and the groin. Try to keep your back as upright as possible. At first you may find this lowering of the body a challenge. It requires great control, good balance and strong leg muscles, but with practice you will find that you achieve it easily.

04

05

Continued on next page

Finishing sequence/3

06

(06) As you curve your arms inwards and forwards as if around the base of a circle, you are in your lowest stance. Now you have to 'carry the tiger' and 'return to the mountain'.

07

(07) *Very slowly, start to straighten your legs as you lift up 'the tiger'. Try to keep your back as upright as you can.*

Continued on next page

Finishing sequence/4

(08) As you straighten your body, turn your hands over when they reach waist height so that the palms face down.

(09) As you continue to rise up, press down with your hands. The top of your body feels light now, and your lower body and legs firmly rooted – as solid as a mountain.

(10) Finally, rotate your hands so that your palms are innermost. Relax your arms and keep a slight bend in your knees. Relax into the Wu Chi posture. This sequence (07–10) is known as Tai Chi Ending, which always marks the end of any Tai Chi practice.

08

09

10

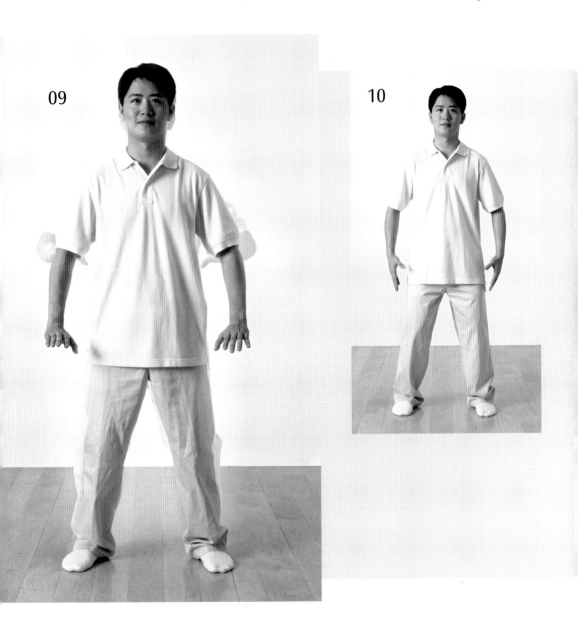

Index

Author's Acknowledgements

I would first like to thank my whole family – my parents and my brothers – for their continuing support and care. My father I need to especially mention and thank for teaching and nourishing my understanding of Tai Chi.

I would also like to extend my gratitude to Jo Godfrey Wood and Camilla Davis, the editors, and Bridget Morley, the designer, for their patience and direct support as this is my first independent work. I would also like to thank Octopus Publishing Group and all the backstage staff for giving me this wonderful opportunity and making this book possible.

Finally, I would like to thank Katherine Rich and my brother, Tin Hun Lam, for modelling in this book.